Stolen

John Wilson

Orca Currents

ORCA BOOK PUBLISHERS

Library and Archives Canada Cataloguing in Publication

Wilson, John (John Alexander), 1951-
Stolen / John Wilson.
(Orca currents)

Issued also in electronic formats.
ISBN 978-1-4598-0376-3 (bound).--ISBN 978-1-4598-0375-6 (pbk.)

I. Title. II. Series: Orca currents
PS8595.I5834S86 2013   jC813'.54   C2012-907489-6

First published in the United States, 2013
Library of Congress Control Number: 2012952959

Summary: Fifteen-year-old Sam solves a mystery while
treasure hunting on the Australian coast.

*Orca Book Publishers is dedicated to preserving the environment and has
printed this book on Forest Stewardship Council® certified paper.*

Orca Book Publishers gratefully acknowledges the support for its
publishing programs provided by the following agencies: the Government
of Canada through the Canada Book Fund and the Canada Council for the Arts,
and the Province of British Columbia through the BC Arts Council
and the Book Publishing Tax Credit.

Cover photography by iStockphoto.com
Author photo by Katherine Gordon

ORCA BOOK PUBLISHERS
PO Box 5626, Stn. B
Victoria, BC Canada
V8R 6S4

ORCA BOOK PUBLISHERS
PO Box 468
Custer, WA USA
98240-0468

www.orcabook.com
Printed and bound in Canada.

16 15 14 13 • 4 3 2 1

For Scotty

have split up. Dad wouldn't have accepted a job in Australia, and I'd be back struggling through grade eleven at Dover Bay Secondary.

Not that that would be a bunch of fun. It'd be a gray, rainy January on Vancouver Island, and I'd be fighting to pull myself up to a B in math while trying to handle all the usual garbage that being sixteen in a big high school throws at you. But I'd be with my friends. I'm not a real outgoing person. It takes me a long time to build up a few good friends. Now they're at the other end of the earth, and I'm walking along a beach at Warrnambool, worrying about starting at a fancy private school in Adelaide in a couple of weeks—we have to wear uniforms! And I'll have to begin the find-friends routine all over again. At least it's not cold and rainy here—the weatherman's calling for thirty-eight degrees this afternoon.

But hot weather doesn't do anything for loneliness.

I kick an old piece of black driftwood ahead of me. I'm walking along the edge of a line of grass-covered sand dunes. To my left, the featureless beach stretches down to where the ocean waves roll in, foaming and crashing as if angry that they can't climb higher toward me. Beyond that, there's nothing until you reach Antarctica. At least there's somewhere more boring than Warrnambool.

I catch up with the piece of driftwood and give it another kick. That's when I hear the counting—"3.141592653589793…" Well, it's not really counting, because the numbers aren't in any sequence I can spot.

I look around. The voice must be coming from behind the dunes. As far as I can see in either direction along the beach, there's only one old guy and his dog. Neither of them is counting.

3

I stumble through the soft sand up the dune face. Normally, I wouldn't go looking for someone talking to themselves, but the numbers are so weird. They're still going on and making no more sense—"…238462643383279…"

At the top of the dune, I see the girl. She's not tough to spot. Bright red hair like hers would stand out a mile away. She's sitting cross-legged in the hollow between my dune and the next one. She is wearing green cargo pants and a loose, long-sleeved khaki shirt. There's a tattered blue backpack beside her. Her eyes are closed and she is still listing numbers—"…5028841971…" Have I stumbled upon a lunatic escaped from a local asylum? Maybe she's part of a coven, and she's chanting a mystical formula to raise the devil. I'm about to return to the beach when the girl stops counting, opens her eyes and stares up at me.

"Hello," she says, without a hint of embarrassment.

"Hello," I reply. Then my throat and brain dry up. Like I said, I'm not an outgoing person. Fortunately, the girl is.

"I was just sitting here reciting Pi," she says, standing, brushing sand off her pants and picking up her backpack.

"Pie?" I ask.

"Sure," she says, coming up the dune toward me. "You know—Pi, the basis of everything."

"Oh, you mean Pi, the mathematical number."

The girl smiles, and I feel my cheeks flush. "My name's Annabel." She arrives at my side and holds out a hand.

I shake it. "I'm Sam." Up close, she is striking. Her hair falls straight halfway down her back and almost glows in the low sun. Her eyes are an odd gray color and stare at me confidently. Her mouth curls up on one side, making it look as if she is permanently amused by something. She's a good four inches taller than me, and I'm only a couple of inches under six feet.

Like a mouse mesmerized by a snake, I stare up at her until she looks down, and I realize I'm still holding her hand. I drop it hurriedly and mumble, "Why were you saying Pi out loud?"

"Because it's cool. Do you want to hear me recite it?"

"Okay," I say, not entirely sure that I do.

Annabel closes her eyes and rattles off numbers, much faster than before. "3.14159265358979323846264338327 95028841971693993751058209749444 592307816406286…"

"That's impressive," I say, interrupting the flow that sounds as if it could go on all day.

Annabel opens her eyes. "I can keep going," she offers.

"That's okay. How many digits have you learned?"

"I'm up to three thousand two hundred and thirty."

"Wow," I say, partly in awe and partly in realization that my guess about an escapee from a lunatic asylum was correct. "That's a lot of numbers."

"It's my party trick." She laughs out loud. "I don't go to many parties. Actually, it's not a lot of digits. The world record for memorizing Pi is over a hundred thousand."

I frown, trying to imagine someone wanting to memorize that many numbers.

"I don't think I'll ever manage that," Annabel says. "My dream is to have Pi tattooed on my arm." She holds out an incredibly long right arm and stares at it. "In a spiral." She twists her left hand in a sinuous motion down the length of the arm. "I reckon I could get several thousand numbers on there. Don't you?"

"I guess so," I say, wondering if I should turn and run for it.

"You're new here," she says, dropping her arm and turning those gray eyes on me. All thoughts of running vanish.

"Yeah," I reply. "My dad's working in Adelaide, so he thought it would be a good idea to drive down here for a holiday for a few days."

"You don't think it's a good idea?"

"The beach is okay," I say defensively, "but there's nothing to do. The town's boring."

"Have you been up Flagstaff Hill?"

"Why would I want to see a flagstaff?"

"There's a museum there. This stretch of coast is called the Shipwreck Coast. Dozens of ships have sunk along here." She waves an arm expansively to take in the entire coast and ocean.

"The museum has all kinds of cool stuff salvaged from wrecks."

"Boring old stuff," I say dismissively, trying to sound casual. I immediately regret it. Annabel's face darkens in anger.

"Boring old stuff!" she says. "You just dismissed all of history. You think people who lived in the past weren't as interesting as you? They were certainly smarter." Annabel strides off down the sand dune.

Chapter Two

The dramatic effect of Annabel's departure is spoiled by the sand dune. Her feet sink and slide into the soft sand, and she waves her arms around wildly for balance.

"Wait," I shout, not wanting the only interesting person I've met here to escape, even if she is insane. "I'm sorry. I like history. Socials is my favorite subject—at least, the bits about battles and rebellions." I manage to stop before saying that math is my least favorite subject—not a smart thing to say to someone who loves Pi.

Annabel stops on the flat part of the beach and waits while I slither down the slope. "You really think history's interesting?" she asks.

"Sure," I say. "Maybe I'll go and check the museum out."

"I work there on the holidays. I could show you round." We start walking back along the beach. "There's lots of great stories about the coast here. The museum has the *Loch Ard* peacock," Annabel says as if I should know what she's talking about.

"Ummmm," I say helplessly.

"It's part of the *Loch Ard* shipwreck. Fifty-two people drowned back in 1878."

"I'm afraid it wasn't big news up in Canada. Do you know about the

Princess Sophia shipwreck? Three hundred and forty-three people drowned back in 1918." I'm dredging up information from a project I did last year. I know I sound pompous, but Annabel's assumption that I should know the history of her backwoods part of the world annoys me.

To my great relief, Annabel laughs. "Fair enough. Tell me about the *Princess Sophia*."

"She was a steamer out on Canada's west coast. She struck a reef in a storm and sank." Annabel looks at me as if she wants more information. "The *Sophia* sat on the reef for two days with rescue ships around her and the weather too rough to take the passengers off. Then she slid off the reef, and everyone drowned. I imagine what it must have been like for the people on board, knowing they were probably going to die but not knowing when. Some wrote last letters and wills that were found when their bodies drifted ashore days later."

Annabel tilts her head and looks at me with interest. "That's powerful stuff. A lot of people forget that history's about people just like us. You haven't."

I feel my neck redden at the compliment. "So tell me about the *Loch Ard*," I say.

"The *Loch Ard* was heading for Melbourne from England with immigrant families aboard. She was swept onto the cliffs along the coast in fog and sank in ten minutes. Only two eighteen-year-olds survived, Tom Pearce, an apprentice, and Eva Carmichael, the daughter of one of the families. Tom was washed ashore, but he heard Eva call for help and swam back out to rescue her. They sheltered in a cave and drank brandy that had washed up.

Then Tom climbed the cliffs and went for help. It was a huge story back then. Everyone hoped Tom and Eva would fall in love. They didn't. Eva went back to Ireland, and Tom was given a gold medal for his bravery. So much for romance.

"Lots of stuff washed up on the beach in the days after the sinking. One thing was a huge porcelain bird specially made in England for the Melbourne exhibition to be held in 1880. That's the *Loch Ard* peacock, and it's in the museum on Flagstaff Hill. They say it's worth millions of dollars."

"I'd like to see that," I say, impressed by the dollar figure.

"There's another fascinating story much closer to here—" Annabel begins, but she stops as the black piece of driftwood that I had been kicking along the beach bounces past us. It comes to rest a few feet away, and Annabel freezes, staring at it. Then she bends down to pick it up, but a large black dog shoots past, grabs the wood and bounds away.

"Hey! Wait!" Annabel shouts and takes off after the dog.

Annabel is tearing around after the dog, who thinks this is a wonderful game, when the dog's owner shows up. "Sorry," he says in an American accent. He's a plump, middle-aged man wearing a dark suit and city shoes that look completely out of place on the beach. He peers at me through thick, round glasses. "The wood slipped out of my hand when I threw it for Percy. There's not a lot of driftwood on this beach, so it's quite a treat for him."

Annabel can cover a lot of ground fast on her long legs, but Percy beats her in the turn every time. As Annabel begins to slow, Percy runs rings round her. "This seems like quite a treat for Percy too," I say.

"Yes," the man agrees, "although I'm not so sure it is for your friend. Are you here on holiday?"

"Just for a few days, yes," I reply. "You're American?"

"Not hard to spot," the man acknowledges with a smile. "From Kansas originally, like Dorothy in *The Wizard of Oz*, but I travel a lot. But with that accent, you're not from hereabouts either."

"I'm Canadian," I explain. "My dad just moved to Adelaide."

Eventually, Annabel stops running and bends over, her hands on her knees. After a final couple of circuits around the gasping girl, Percy loses interest. He drops the wood and trots back to his master. Annabel comes back to life, grabs the driftwood and examines it closely.

I scratch Percy behind the ear as he snuffles up to me to say hello. "Sorry again," the man says. "Nice meeting you. Come on, Percy. Time to go home."

As they wander off down the beach, I wonder why they're heading away from town, but Annabel and her old piece of wood distract me. I trot over to see what's so interesting.

"That looked like fun," I say. Annabel ignores me. "What's so fascinating about an old bit of wood?"

"Sam," Annabel says, staring at the dunes behind us. "How much driftwood do you see on this beach?"

I glance up and down. "None," I say.

"Exactly. So where did this piece come from?"

I shrug.

Annabel looks at me and holds out the wood. It's not much bigger than my clenched fist and slightly longer than it is wide. The ends are jagged, but one side is straight, like it was made by a tool. "It's man-made and it's black," she says.

I'm tempted to point out that I've worked that out already, but instead

I say, "What does that mean? It could have come from anywhere. You said this was the shipwreck coast."

"That's true, but there's the story I was going to tell you before Percy interrupted us. There is supposed to be a lost ship buried in the dunes somewhere around here. It was first seen in the early1800s, and on and off for about 80 years after that. No one's seen it since 1880, and there are all sorts of theories about what it was. A lot of people think it might prove that someone from Europe or Asia came to Australia before Willem Janszoon landed here in 1606."

"Janszoon?"

"He was a Dutch explorer. Most people think he was the first European to visit Australia, although he didn't know that's where he was."

"So why should Percy's bit of wood be from that wreck and not another one?"

"The one thing that everyone who saw the wreck agrees on is that the ship was constructed out of black wood," Annabel explains. "That's unusual. People call it the Mahogany Ship."

"So we've found an ancient, mysterious wreck," I say, my interest piqued now.

"Not necessarily. Even if this is from the Mahogany Ship, it doesn't tell us where the wreck is. It could be buried under meters of sand. But what we *can* do"—Annabel smiles and stuffs the wood into her backpack—"is take this up to the museum and see if anyone there can tell us anything about it. You up for it?"

"Sure," I say as we head off down the beach. Suddenly, Warrnambool isn't as boring as I thought.

Chapter Three

The walk back into town is hot, and Annabel shares a drink from the water bottle in her backpack. We walk along the beach, through town and into the museum on top of Flagstaff Hill. Annabel nods to the girl selling tickets. "Hi, Penny. Busy day?"

"Wish it was," Penny answers. "Busy makes the time go faster."

Annabel chuckles, and we pass through a door marked *Staff Only*.

We're in a short corridor with two doors on either side. A plate on the first door on the right announces *Rose MacAuley, Director of Artifact and Building Preservation and Park Maintenance*.

"Rose is a wonder," Annabel says. "She does everything—makes sure the old buildings in the heritage park out back don't fall down, keeps the museum exhibits clean and prepares new finds for display."

The second door has a plate saying *William Sturridge, Director of Research*. Annabel knocks on that door, but there's no reply. "Bill must be at lunch," she says, looking at her watch. "Probably with Rose."

We continue down the corridor into an open room with views over the ocean. There's a simple kitchen setup, a couch and an assortment of chairs arranged around an oval table. The young man sitting at one end of the table looks up from his tablet as we enter.

"G'day, Anna. I was just checking out a new zombie game. You want to have a look? You can make their heads explode."

I feel Annabel tense beside me, and I take an instant dislike to the man. He's skinny and twitchy. He taps his foot as his eyes flit back and forth between Annabel and me. It makes me restless just looking at him.

"Well done, Pete," Annabel says coldly. "Just when I thought you couldn't get any more disgusting, you outdo yourself."

Pete flashes a smile that's closer to a sneer. "Where you been this morning?"

"As if it's any of your business, it's my day off," Annabel replies as we sit down as far from Pete as possible. "And I've told you before, just because you shorten your name doesn't mean that everyone does. My name's Annabel."

"Sure, sure," Pete says with a dismissive wave. "And who's your new friend?"

"That also is none of your business, but his name's Sam."

Pete smirks. "Short for Samuel, I suppose. Pleased to meet you, Sam."

"Hi," I say, feeling intensely uncomfortable.

We all sit in silence for a few minutes. Then Pete speaks, "Say, Anna—Annabel, sorry. Have you had a chance to ask Bill about putting me on night shift?"

"Not yet," Annabel says. "Why are you so keen to go on night shift?"

"It'd be cool. No one to hassle me or tell me what to do. Maybe you'd like to join me one night."

"In your dreams. Has anyone ever told you what a creep you are?"

"Many people," Pete says with his sneering smile, "but I'm only kidding. Seriously, will you have a word with Bill?"

"Yeah, okay. At least it would get you off the same shifts as me."

"Thanks, babe."

I can see Annabel gritting her teeth, but she says, "Have Bill and Rose gone for lunch?"

"Should be back soon. You can ask him about my night shift when he gets back. You want to see this?" Pete waves his tablet in my direction.

Before I can think of an answer, Annabel stands up. "Come on," she says. "I want to show you something while we're waiting."

"Can I see it too?" Pete asks, in a tone that suggests he's not talking about a museum artifact.

Annabel ignores him, and we head back down the corridor and through the gift shop. "He's such a slime bag," she says as soon as we're out of hearing range. "He sends shivers down my spine every time I talk to him. I don't know why Bill hired him."

"Maybe he'll be put on the night shift," I suggest. "Then he'll be out of your way."

"I should be so lucky. We had a security guy on night shift, an old Vietnam veteran, but he got sick and had to quit. Bill's hired a security firm now."

"Why does Pete ask you to talk to Bill? Why doesn't he approach him himself?"

"Bill's my uncle," Annabel explains. "Pete reckons I have influence with him. I've been stalling because I don't want to do Pete any favors, but it *would* be good to get rid of him."

We're in the museum now, sur-rounded by glass cases full of cracked plates, barnacle-encrusted jars and photographs of old sailing ships. I have to admit that some of it looks interesting, but Annabel doesn't give me a chance to linger. She leads me to the museum's back door and out onto a balcony overlooking a clutter of buildings that covers a hill sloping down to the sea.

"This is our heritage village," she says proudly.

"Is this the original Warrnambool?"

"No. The buildings are all original, but not from one place. The museum has collected them from all over. They rescued them from developers in some cases and brought them here to recreate what an ideal town might have looked like a hundred and fifty years ago. There are houses, a church, a school, a blacksmith shop, a store…"

"And ships," I say, looking down at a pond in which a sailing ship and an old-fashioned ferry are floating. There's also a dock with a red rowboat tied at the end.

"It's an old lagoon that used to be attached to the sea. The two-masted ketch is the *Reginald M—Reggie* for short. He was built in 1922 and worked as a freighter all along this coast. The steamship is *Rowitta*. She was built in 1909 and was used for tourist excursions on the Tamar River in Tasmania. I'll show you around later, but right now I want you to see the star of the show."

I follow Annabel back into the museum and through to an open circular area. The usual cases are around the walls, but there's a tall, circular glass case in the middle that makes me gasp in surprise. I glance at Annabel, who's smiling at my shock. "Impressive, eh?" she says.

I'm looking at a peacock. On its pedestal, it is taller than I am. I walk around it. It's perfect—the feathers on the tail are painted in incredible detail, the eyes real enough to be looking at me, the talons curled to grip the rock on which it stands, the blues, greens and browns so bright, they almost hurt my eyes. It looks about to spread its magnificent tail and strut majestically out the door. "It's beautiful," I say.

"Hard to believe it's made out of porcelain," Annabel says. "Only nine of these were ever made," she goes on, sounding like a tour guide. "It's 144 centimeters high and weighs 45.36 kilos, and it's insured for four million dollars."

"Wait a minute. If this thing is porcelain, how did it survive a shipwreck that killed almost everyone on board?"

"It was so special that it wasn't put in the hold. It was packed very carefully in a crate and stored in the captain's cabin. When the *Loch Ard* went down, the captain did as well, but the crate with the peacock inside floated onto the beach."

"It's a miracle it survived."

"Indeed it is." I turn to see a tall bearded man striding toward us. "Hi, Annabel," he says. "Pete told me you were here."

"This is Sam," Annabel says, and Bill and I shake hands. "I was just showing him the *Loch Ard* peacock."

"Our pride and joy," Bill says. "This brings the tourists in, but a lot of the less dramatic stuff is more important for the archaeologist. An old shoe or a dinner service can tell us more about people's lives a hundred years ago than something like this."

"Something like this, maybe?" Annabel asks as she pulls the piece of black wood from her backpack.

Bill examines it with interest, moving over to the glass door to get better light. "Where did you find this?"

"Down on the beach, a couple of kilometers west of town."

"Is it mahogany?" I blurt out. I'm surprised how much I want this old bit of wood to be important. If it is, it'll be an excuse to hang out with Annabel.

Bill laughs. "You think this is part of the Mahogany Ship?"

"Maybe," I say, feeling sheepish at his laugh.

"It's oak," Bill says. Then, seeing disappointment cross my face, he adds, "It's unlikely that the Mahogany Ship was actually made of mahogany. Someone called it that because the wood was black, but a lot of wood turns black if it's buried.

"It's obviously from a wreck," Bill goes on, turning his attention back to the wood. "Possibly a piece of a rudder post, but there's not enough to tell for sure."

"So it could be from the Mahogany Ship?" I ask excitedly.

Bill laughs again. "I see it hasn't taken you long to get involved in our local legends. Yes, it could be from the Mahogany Ship—if it exists—but it's more likely that it's from one of the other wrecks along the coast. There were dozens over the years, from large ships like the *Loch Ard* to small fishing boats. Of course, there's no way to tell for sure, which is why the mystery of the Mahogany Ship has lasted so long."

"That's kind of what I thought," Annabel says, "but, hey, you never know, right?"

"You never know," Bill repeats with a smile. "Let me hang on to this, and I'll let you know if I have any other thoughts. Are you going back to look for more pieces?"

I look at Annabel. "Of course," she says, "but not today—it'll be too hot this afternoon."

"They say a big storm is coming through tonight," Bill adds. "Unusual for this time of year, but we've had a lot of unusual weather lately."

"If it clears up tomorrow, we'll go and poke around," Annabel says. "If you want to?" she asks me.

"Sure," I say, trying to keep the excitement out of my voice. There's nothing I'd rather do than spend the day on the beach with Annabel.

"Great," Bill says. "Bring me back some Spanish gold or pirate treasure for the museum. Why don't you take Sam down and show him our village?"

"I will, but I thought we might grab a Coke in the cafeteria first."

"Good idea. Nice meeting you, Sam." Bill shakes my hand.

"And you," I reply.

Bill turns away, but Annabel stops him. "I almost forgot. Pete asked me to ask you to put him on the night shift."

"To get him away from you?" Bill asks. "You don't like him, do you?"

"Honestly? I can't stand him," Annabel says. "He's crude and rude."

"He is a bit full of himself," Bill agrees, "but he does his work. I'll think about the night-shift idea. The security firm we have now is good, but they're expensive, and we can't afford to keep paying them forever. Pete might work over the summer until we can hire someone better."

Bill heads to his office, and, with a last glance at the *Loch Ard* peacock, Annabel and I head for the cafeteria.

Chapter Four

About two in the morning, I wake up
convinced that the cabin Dad and I
have rented is about to blow into the
ocean. The walls are creaking, and
the glass in the windows is making
a threatening, thumping sound. The
storm has arrived.

I open the front door and peer
through the screen in time to see a tent

bounce by. The lights that normally illu-
minate the park at night are out, but it
makes little difference because the light-
ning is nonstop, and the thunder feels as
if it's coming from the ground beneath
my feet. The rain lashes across the scene
horizontally, and there are small rivers
running over the open ground.

"Wild night, eh?" Dad says over my
shoulder.

"Yeah," I agree.

"Shouldn't last long. Storms like this
are unusual at this time of year."

Yesterday I might have said, "How
do you know?" But today I keep silent.
Dad has this habit of becoming an
instant expert. As soon as he accepted
the job in Adelaide, he knew everything about the city and Australia. It had
triggered numerous shouting matches
before we moved. What I was really
shouting about, though, was the move to
Australia. Now that I've met Annabel,

I am less inclined to get into a fight about being here.

"Are you feeling better about our move?" Dad asks.

"I suppose so," I reply. Annabel gave me the web address for the museum yesterday, and I read every word it had on the history of the coast. "This place seems to be more interesting than I thought. Though I can't say I'm honestly looking forward to the new school." I hold up my hand to stop Dad from launching into an explanation of why it's the best school in South Australia. "I know. I'll manage."

Dad smiles more broadly than I've seen in a while.

The screen door vibrates loudly, and I look back out at the storm. "It'll all work out," I say. "Australia's not so bad."

Dad pats me on the shoulder. "Assuming we don't all get washed away in the storm."

"I hear they don't last long at this time of year," I say.

Dad grins and goes back to bed, and I watch the storm a bit longer.

The next morning I look at the sky and think how one would never know how bad the weather was just a few hours before. The sky is a cloudless, washed-out blue, as if all the rain has left it exhausted.

The ground is a different story. The campsite looks like a war zone. Tents are collapsed or ripped, and camping equipment litters the ground. Most campers took refuge in the large communal kitchen area and are now emerging to survey the damage. The water has carved what looks like a miniature Grand Canyon across the volleyball court.

I feel sorry for the people who have had a miserable night, but I'm happy despite that. The storm has passed, and the weather isn't going to stop my meeting Annabel and searching for more relics. Actually, relics of mysterious ships would be a bonus—I'm mainly looking forward to a day with my new friend.

I have breakfast with Dad, who says he's disappointed I won't be spending the day with him, but I know that he's brought work from his new job with him, so he'll be quite happy. I unlock my bike and head off. Annabel and I have decided to take bikes today so that we can cover more ground. Behind the dunes there's a track that runs parallel to the beach, and we can use it to access the areas we want to explore.

I meet Annabel on the edge of town. "Quite the storm last night," she says.

"It caused havoc in the campsite. Tents blown all over the place, and we won't be playing volleyball for a while."

"Yeah, it did some damage in town too. Brought down some trees, and the power's still out in some places. The museum's closed today."

"Was it damaged?"

"Oh no, but an electrical short blew out the security system about two AM. Pete's there organizing the electricians, and Penny's helping keep an eye on the place. There were a lot of power outages last night, so it was tough to find anyone to fix it this morning, but we can't leave the museum unprotected."

"I guess not."

Annabel hops on her bike and pedals down the trail.

"Do we start searching on the beach?" I shout after her.

"No. There's been a change of plan," Annabel calls over her shoulder.

"Why?" I ask as I pedal hard to catch up.

"Because of the storm last night. Bill called me and said to meet him down the coast." It's slow going on the uneven path, but it's wide enough for us to cycle side by side and talk.

"Has he found something?" I ask.

"He wouldn't say. Told me to wait and see."

"Have you learned any more digits for Pi?" I ask, to keep the conversation going.

Annabel laughs. "Not since yesterday. But I am planning a Pi Day party."

"A what party?"

"A Pi Day party. Pi Day is March 14. To be precise, celebrations occur at 1:59 AM."

"What are you talking about?" I ask, thoroughly confused.

"March is the third month, and three point one four is the approximation of Pi that Archimedes worked out."

"Let me guess," I say. "One, five, nine are the next three numbers."

"Exactly," Annabel says, her voice rising with enthusiasm. "And you know what else?"

"What?" I ask. This is really weird, and I'm struggling to understand what Annabel's telling me while staying on the path.

"March 14 is Einstein's birthday."

"Wow. I'm so glad I asked. And what do people do on Pi Day?"

"Eat pie, of course," Annabel says with a laugh.

"You're such a nerd," I say. I immediately regret it, but Annabel doesn't seem to mind.

"I'm not a nerd," she says, "I'm a geek."

"There's a difference?"

"'Course there's a difference. Nerds were invented by Dr. Seuss. They're obsessed, boring, unpopular people who are often stupid."

"And you're not obsessed?"

"Okay, I'm obsessed," Annabel admits. "And maybe I'm a bit boring, but I'm not stupid. Geeks are intelligent, knowledgeable and accomplished."

"You're such a geek," I correct myself.

"The original geeks were carnival performers who did weird stuff like biting the heads off live chickens."

I really don't have a response to that, but Annabel's on a roll. "You know what else?" she asks.

"No," I reply nervously.

"I brought us pie for lunch."

Chapter Five

Annabel stands on her pedals and bursts forward. I follow, and we shoot out into a sandy parking lot where two beat-up pickup trucks are parked.

"Here we are," Annabel announces, braking hard and jumping off her bike.

I dump my bike and notice two things. First, one of the trucks has a Flagstaff Hill Museum sticker on the door.

Second, the path we've been cycling along ends in an eroded canyon much bigger than the one in the campsite. "That's some canyon," I say.

"It's an erosion gully," Annabel replies. "Too much rain all at once. It has to go somewhere, so it cuts down into the ground wherever it's soft enough."

"Is this where Bill said to meet him?" I ask, but Annabel is already on her way toward the beach. I follow her down the path and up a large dune to where two figures are deep in conversation. One of them is Bill. He waves cheerfully as we approach.

"Good morning," he says. "You took your time."

"I had to pick up Sam," Annabel says.

My first view is of the beach, where huge rollers, a relic of last night's storm, are crashing onto the sand. Then I turn around and see why we are up here.

The erosion gully is much bigger here—I guess at least nine feet wide and almost as deep. The walls are steep, and tiny avalanches of sand cascade down occasionally. About sixteen feet away, near the bottom of the gully, several thick black pieces of curved timber are sticking out of the bank.

"Is that—" I begin.

"The Mahogany Ship?" Annabel finishes my sentence for me. "Yes, it is."

"Let's not jump to conclusions," Bill says. "There are dozens of wrecks along here."

"Who's this?" The man beside Bill asks. He's short and sturdy with weather-beaten skin and watery blue eyes. He's wearing dirty work clothes and a battered and stained, wide-brimmed bush hat. He looks angry. "We don't want to turn this into a circus. The fewer who know, the better."

"He's a friend of Annabel's," Bill says. "Sam, meet Jim Kelly. Pete's father."

"Pleased to meet you." I hold out my hand and Kelly shakes it reluctantly.

"As I was saying," Bill goes on, "this could be one of any number of wrecks."

Kelly snorts derisively. "I've been searching for the Mahogany Ship for twenty years," he says loudly and aggressively, as if challenging people to disagree with him. "It's exactly where I said it would be."

"Even if this is the Mahogany Ship," Bill says calmly, "it doesn't prove that anyone was here before Janszoon in 1606. There are countless possible wrecks this could be."

Kelly clears his throat and spits on the sand. "You know as well as I do that there's no record of ships lost along here that fit this description. This is the Mahogany Ship, and it's either a

Portuguese caravel or a Chinese junk from hundreds of years before Janszoon."

"Well," Bill says, "we could argue all day, but whatever this is, we have to examine it while we can. This gully is unstable. We don't have a lot of time." He begins taking photographs with a small camera he's pulled from his pocket.

I feel something rub against my leg and look down to see a black dog wagging its tail and looking up at me. "Hello, Percy. What're you doing here?"

"Out for a morning walk." We all look up to see Percy's owner cresting the dune above the beach. He's out of breath and looks even more out of place in his suit here than he did on the beach yesterday. "Some storm last night."

"Why don't we just invite the whole town out to have a look?" Kelly mutters under his breath.

"What do we have here?" Percy's master asks as he joins our little group.

"Did the storm uncover something interesting for the museum?"

"Just a few bits of wood," Bill says. "We won't know what it is until we look closer."

"Excellent. Excellent," the man says. "Good luck with it. Nice to see you again," he says to me. "Come on, Percy. Let's go find some breakfast."

The pair sets off toward the parking lot. The man nods to Annabel, who has walked over to the edge of the gully opposite the black timbers. She is staring intently into the gully.

"Do you see something?" Bill asks.

"I think so," she shouts back, taking a step forward.

"Annabel, keep away from the edge. It's unstable," Bill yells.

"It's okay. I think I can get down here." Annabel steps to the edge, sits and slides down into the gully, disappearing from our view. We all run to where she was and look down. She's standing in the bottom of the gully, waving up to us. "The edge has already slumped in here, so it's not that steep."

"But it's dangerous," Bill says. "The sand's still wet, but as it dries there'll be more slumps. Come back out."

"I will," Annabel replies, "in a minute." She turns away from us, crouches down and begins digging around something in the sand beside the lowest piece of black timber.

"Come back up!" Bill orders.

"I've almost got it," Annabel replies without turning round. "It looks like a—"

Without warning, the entire bank above Annabel collapses, and she vanishes beneath a pile of sand. Without thinking, I leap over the edge and slither and stumble down. I ignore the others shouting behind me and dig frantically with my bare hands.

Chapter Six

How long can someone survive buried like this? I know it's a long time in a snow avalanche. But this is wet, heavy sand. There are no air pockets in it. How long does it take a person to suffocate? Five minutes? Six minutes? What if I'm digging in the wrong place? Things are happening painfully slowly, but my brain is racing. How long has it been?

The voices from above sound very far away. Then Bill is beside me, shouting, "Get the shovels from the truck."

My arms are aching already. The middle finger on my left hand hurts. I think I've torn the nail off. I don't stop. I ignore the pain and keep digging. How long can I keep this up? I keep scratching, digging, throwing.

My hand hits something sharp. I have a moment of wild hope. But it is only the broken end of the black wood that Annabel had crouched beside.

"She's over here," I yell and move a foot and a half to my right. Bill's and my hands keep hitting each other, we're working so close together. I can hear him gasping for breath as he digs feverishly. I realize I am breathless too. My lungs hurt almost as much as my arms do.

My hand gets entangled in some buried seaweed or grass. I yank it angrily. It comes up clutching a bunch of red hair.

It takes me a moment to recognize what I have.

"I've found her." I scream it, even though Bill is right beside me. The hair's all over the place. Bill reaches Annabel's forehead. We scoop sand away.

She must have looked up when the wall above her collapsed. We soon have her face clear. I almost faint with relief when she gags weakly and spits out a mouthful of sand.

"Here's the shovels." I look up and see Kelly standing on the edge. Two shovels slide down and bump to rest beside us.

"Thank you," Bill shouts. "Do you have any water?"

A one-liter plastic bottle bounces down. I rip the lid off and pour the water over Annabel's sandy face. I laugh out loud when she complains, "Hey."

"Are you okay?" I ask. I know it's a stupid question, but I'm not thinking clearly.

"Do I...look okay?" Annabel replies, gasping for breath.

"Have you broken anything?" Bill's question is much more sensible than mine.

"I don't...think so." Annabel's taking shallow, short gasps for breath. "Tight...around my...chest...and my leg's...sore...but okay. No need to... tear my hair out."

"Sorry," I gasp.

"Hang in there," Bill says. "We'll have you out in no time."

Bill and I start digging around Annabel. A lot of sand came down, and Bill keeps looking nervously at the bank above us. Once we've got dug down a bit, Annabel manages to free her right arm and help. When her chest is free, her breathing becomes easier.

"I'm going to try and haul you out," Bill says. We've dug almost to Annabel's waist. The sand keeps sliding back into the hole as we dig, and it's only going to get worse the deeper we go.

"Okay," Annabel says.

Bill crouches down and grasps Annabel under her armpits. He pauses for second, takes a deep breath and hauls. Nothing happens. I start scraping sand away with my shovel.

"Careful with that," Annabel says. "I don't want to survive being buried alive just to have you hack me to bits with a shovel." She sounds cheerful enough, but I saw her grimace in pain when Bill pulled.

"See how far you can get reciting Pi before we get you out," I suggest.

"The way you guys are going, I'll break the world record," she says, but she begins, "3.141592653589793…"

We dig a bit more and then Bill tries again. This time Annabel moves. I work as hard as I can to scrape sand away. Bill pulls a third time. With a scream,

Annabel comes free, and we all fall back against the far wall. Sand cascades around us.

"Come on," Bill says. "Let's get out of here."

Half carrying Annabel between us, we head toward the parking lot, where the gully is shallower. Eventually, we climb out and pull Annabel up after us. We sit gasping beside one of the trucks.

"You didn't get very far with Pi," I say.

"You guys are too good for me," Annabel says with a wry smile. Sucking air through her teeth, she flexes her right leg.

"Is it broken?" Bill asks.

"I don't think so," Annabel replies. "It was bent under me with my weight and all that sand on top of it. I think it's just bruised or strained."

"That was a stupid thing to do," Bill says, but his voice has no anger in it.

"I know," Annabel says with a smile, "but look what I found." She holds out her left hand. Nestled in the palm is a plain, softball-sized clay pot. "This is what I saw beside the black timber. It looked different, so I went down to get it."

She hands the pot to Bill, who turns it over and examines it thoughtfully. "It's old. No doubt about that." The pot is cracked but looks as if it's held together by some kind of rust and there's sand encrusted over much of it. I peer into the mouth, but it's only more rust and sand.

"Do you think it's from the Mahogany Ship?" I ask.

"Could be," Bill says.

"You okay?" We look up to see Kelly heading toward us.

"Yeah, we're fine," Bill replies, slipping the pot into his pocket.

"What was it she went tearing down there to find?" Kelly asks.

"That's the last thing on my mind right now," Bill replies.

"Anyway, you got out just in time. The walls are collapsing fast. It'll be awhile before we see the Mahogany Ship again. At least we've proved it's here."

"Maybe," Bill says, standing up. "But it's more important to get Annabel to the hospital."

I lean on my left hand to stand up and collapse with a cry of pain. My middle fingernail is gone, and the end of the finger is raw and bloody. And there's a gash on the ball of my thumb where the broken end of the wood has cut me. It doesn't appear to be bleeding, but that's probably only because the wound is packed with sand.

"Looks like you need to get to the hospital as well," Bill says. He helps me up and the three of us stumble toward the truck. "I'm going to call Heritage Victoria and tell them about the find,"

Bill shouts back to Kelly. "Don't do anything dumb while I'm gone."

Kelly doesn't reply. Bill loads our bikes into the back of the truck, and we climb into the cab. As we head out of the parking lot, I see Percy and his master in the distance, heading along the path toward town. They must really love walking—it's a good two or three miles back to the edge of town.

As Bill drives, Annabel leans against my shoulder. "Thank you," she whispers. I'm filthy, I ache all over, and my hand is torn and bleeding, but I'm happier than I've been in months.

Chapter Seven

"You are extremely lucky. Sand is basically moving rock, and it's just as heavy. Every year, kids die because they dig tunnels in sand and it collapses on them. If it wasn't for the quick response of your friends, we wouldn't be having this conversation." The doctor is looking at Annabel, who is propped up in a bed in the emergency department of the Warrnambool hospital. She's been cleaned up, examined, x-rayed and declared fit. She'll have a limp for a few days from the bruising to her leg and sore ribs from breathing against the weight of sand, but nothing is broken.

While Annabel was being tested and prodded, another doctor cleaned and stitched the cut on my hand and bandaged my finger where the nail used to be. Bill went off to make phone calls.

"Just take some Ibuprofen for the pain and you'll be good in a day or two. And don't do anything that dumb again." The doctor smiles, flips the curtain back and leaves.

"Thank you," Annabel calls after the doctor. "And thank you." She turns to me with a smile that makes my knees go weak. "You saved my life."

"What was I going to do?" I ask. "Let your skeleton become part of the

Mahogany Ship? That would just mess with archaeologists a hundred years from now. Besides, I haven't heard how far you can go with this Pi thing."

Annabel's lopsided grin broadens. "3.1415…"

"Enough!" I say with a laugh. I'm still amazed at how easy it is to talk and joke with Annabel. Normally, I'm tongue-tied and awkward, especially around beautiful girls. It takes me a long time to get comfortable in anyone's company, but I feel as if I've known Annabel all my life.

"Do you feel up to going and grabbing a Coke?" I ask.

"Sure," Annabel replies. "Bill is probably down in the cafeteria making his phone calls."

I help Annabel limp downstairs and get us a Coke and a donut each. We see Bill outside on his cell, pacing back and forth. He throws me a quick wave.

As I carry our snacks to the table, I think back to the beach. "Bill said that Kelly is Pete's father," I say. "What was he doing down on the beach this morning?"

"Jim Kelly's the local shipwreck nut," Annabel says. "He's got more stuff in his house than we have in the museum."

"Aren't shipwrecks protected?"

"Only those we know about. Kelly runs a diving business, taking tourists out to well-known wrecks, but who's to say where he dives in his spare time."

"So Kelly just helps himself when he finds something and stores it in his house?"

"There's maybe more to Kelly's work than that. Selling artifacts to rich collectors is a profitable business. It's a thriving trade in Egypt, for example, and it's not just some local goat herder stumbling on a burial urn and selling it to a tourist.

It's well organized and linked to the big crime syndicates. Say you collect ancient Babylonian statues, and there's one you really want. You go to a crooked art dealer, who goes to his crime connection, who goes to the local lads, who steal the statue from a museum.

"The looting of the national museum in Baghdad in 2003 was organized. Thousands of pieces were stolen, and many of the most valuable pieces were targeted. The thieves ignored the replicas on display and used keys to get into vaults where the originals were stored. They knew what they were doing, and someone had probably arranged the sale of the best pieces in advance. In fact, several hundred pieces were found in FedEx boxes in New York, on their way to an American art dealer."

Annabel falls silent and looks sheepish. "Sorry. I tend to get carried away. I didn't mean to lecture you."

"That's okay," I say. "I've learned a lot in the last two days. I'll never be able to look at March 14 the same again."

"Well," Annabel says with a laugh, "I'm glad you're remembering the important stuff."

"Do you think Kelly and Pete are involved in smuggling?"

"Probably only in a small way. Kelly's probably not above selling something if the opportunity arises, but I doubt he's involved with international crime. Besides, apart from the *Loch Ard* peacock, there's not much here to interest a big collector."

"And the peacock would be hard to smuggle out under your jacket."

"It would," Annabel agrees. "Kelly's style is more about finding items no one else has. That's why he's so into the Mahogany Ship, and why he headed out early this morning to see if the storm had uncovered anything."

"Why? The Mahogany Ship might be interesting, but surely any treasure would be gone by now."

"I think it's fame he's after."

"Fame?"

"The person who discovers a wreck that proves someone got to Australia way before Janszoon would be famous. There'd be TV appearances, articles in magazines, a book, maybe even a movie—fame."

"And Kelly thinks the Mahogany Ship will prove someone beat Janszoon here?"

"Probably a Portuguese explorer. They were in Indonesia, not too far away, in the 1500s. There are Portuguese maps that, if you use some imagination, look like bits of the Australian coast. Also, there are mentions of voyages with no official records, either because they were kept secret or because the records were lost."

"You don't sound convinced."

"I'm not. It's like all conspiracy theories. If you believe that multiple assassins shot Kennedy or that 9/11 was an inside job, you'll fill the gaps in the record with whatever crackpot idea you want. How easy is it to do that with something that happened five hundred years ago?"

"I suppose you're right," I say, disappointed by Annabel's rationality. I want the Mahogany Ship to be a real-life mystery. Then I remember something else. "Kelly also said something about a Chinese ship?"

"Most people think the Mahogany Ship's a Portuguese caravel. Kelly imagines he can see the outline of a wreck on the aerial photos and that it's something almost seventy meters long. The largest caravels were only half that size. So he thinks it's a Chinese junk that sailed here a hundred years before even the phantom Portuguese."

"A Chinese junk?" I repeat. "They couldn't sail this far."

"That's not the problem. Between 1405 and 1433, a Chinese admiral called Zheng He made seven voyages with huge fleets of junks. They sailed all around the Indian Ocean and down the African coast. There is evidence that some of the junks got into the Atlantic Ocean and maybe even all the way across the Pacific. Some people think the Chinese got to both coasts of Canada. Some of Zheng He's junks were over a hundred meters long, and they were loaded with treasure to trade with the people he met."

"So the Mahogany Ship could be one of these junks loaded with treasure?" My interest is rekindled.

"Sorry to disappoint you," Annabel says with a smile, "but probably not. The Chinese kept good records, and there's no mention of an expedition in this area."

"What about the old pot you almost died finding? That's old, isn't it?"

"Sure it's old. It might even be Chinese."

My eyes widen at that, but Annabel soon crushes my romantic dreams of treasure ships.

"By old I mean a hundred and fifty years or so, not six hundred. What I found was almost certainly dropped by someone pottering around the old wreck in the nineteenth century, looking for treasure. It might have been a Chinese laborer. There were a lot of them working in the goldfields from the 1850s on."

Annabel laughs at my disappointed expression. "One thing I've learned working for Bill is that archaeology is nothing like Indiana Jones. It's spending days struggling to make an old piece of wood or leather, a pot or a coin tell you a tiny fragment of a story. It's not romantic.

For example, Bill will give the pot I found to Rose, who will take it to her lab and spend hours cleaning, scraping and dissolving to find out what's inside. Then, maybe, she'll be able to say that it was dropped by someone around 1850. Then we can put it in a small corner of our display on the Mahogany Ship. Sorry."

"It's okay," I say, returning her laugh. "I've read too many adventure stories."

I'm feeling wonderfully happy sitting here with Annabel when the cafeteria door flies open and Bill strides toward us. "We have to go," he says in a voice loud and urgent enough to turn the heads of the other cafeteria patrons.

"What is it?" Annabel and I say at the same instant, but Bill's already past us, heading for the parking lot.

"Someone's stolen the *Loch Ard* peacock," he shouts over his shoulder.

"In how many pieces?" Bill asks miserably.

Annabel moves away from the pedestal, crouches down and stares at something on the floor.

"What is it?" I ask, joining her. She seems to be studying the silver lock. The halves of the lock lie side by side. They don't look damaged, but one wouldn't expect them to be, since the thieves shattered the case rather than forcing the lock.

Before Annabel can respond, the police inspector sticks his head around a display. "We're done here," he says. "I've got a couple of officers interviewing the neighbors to see if anyone saw anything suspicious. Forensics is still dusting for prints, so don't touch anything, but as soon as he's done you can begin cleaning up."

"Thank you," Bill says. "Do you have any leads yet?"

"Too early to know. We'll review all the interviews and see what that tells us, and forensics will narrow fingerprints down to those that don't belong to the staff. It'll take time."

"I suppose so," Bill says. "Thanks again."

We move through to the staff room. "Oh, I'm so sorry, Mr. Sturridge," Penny says as we enter. "I should have seen something."

Bill pours himself a coffee and we all sit at the table. "I know you've probably had to tell the police everything three or four times, but could you go over it once more for me?"

"Of course, Mr. Sturridge," Penny says. She's tiny, no more than five feet one or two, and so delicate that she looks more fragile than the peacock did. Her short hair is dyed jet black. Her face is red from crying. "I was just coming out of the washroom when I heard a crash from the museum. I thought some-thing had fallen over, you know, after the storm last night." Penny sniffs and blows her nose loudly.

"Did you go straight through?" Bill asks.

"No, I went back to the front desk to make sure everything was all right there first."

"Was it?" Bill asks.

"Yes. The front doors were locked, and there was no one in the parking lot."

"No suspicious vehicles?"

Penny shakes her head dejectedly. "Then I went though to the museum. It was like you saw it—glass from the smashed case everywhere and the peacock gone. I'm afraid I screamed."

"I would have as well," Annabel says gently. "Were the electricians still here?"

"No. They left about half an hour before I heard the crash. They said the alarms were fixed and not to forget to arm them when we left."

"So it was just you and Pete here?" Bill asked.

"Yes. Ms. MacAuley called in sick."

"I know," Bill said thoughtfully. "She texted me this morning. Did you hear the crash, Pete?"

"I heard Penny scream. I was on the balcony having a smoke. When I came in, she was standing by the broken case."

"And you didn't see anyone suspicious round back?"

"No."

"This is impossible." Bill stands up. He's talking loudly and almost shaking with anger. "The peacock's a meter and a half tall and weighs forty-five kilos. It can't just vanish. I want this entire place searched. Sam, will you help?"

"Of course," I say.

"Good. I'll search the museum. The four of you split up the village. Search every space big enough to hide the peacock. Don't forget *Reggie* and *Rowitta*. I want to be absolutely certain that the peacock's not on this property."

"So, it's not here," Annabel says. We're sitting on *Reggie*'s deck, tired and confused. Penny has gone back up to the museum, and Pete is sitting sullenly on the dock across the pond from us. I have an uncomfortable feeling that something is wrong, but I can't figure out what. Pete flicks a cigarette butt out over the water, stands and, without a glance in our direction, heads back up to the museum.

We have searched every building in the heritage village. Annabel and I have even double-checked some of the buildings in Pete's search area, since we felt he wasn't taking the job seriously. Nothing. We're both certain the peacock isn't hidden anywhere in the village.

"So where is it?" I ask. "Like Bill said, it's impossible."

"It happened, so it's obviously possible," Annabel says. "We just need to think it through rationally."

"Pi's not going to help us here," I say more harshly than I intend.

"Probably not," Annabel says, showing no sign that I have offended her. "But what Pi represents—science, rationalism, clear thinking—will."

"How?" I ask glumly. The excitement from the morning's discovery and Annabel's accident has vanished. It's midafternoon, and it's hot. I'm hungry, thirsty and fed up, and my bandaged hand is throbbing. "Science can't explain everything."

"Maybe the *Loch Ard* peacock was taken by aliens."

I turn and stare at Annabel. She looks serious. "That's ridiculous."

"Hmmm. Perhaps you're right. If aliens can travel across space, they probably have the technology to take the peacock without breaking the case. How about ghosts? A lot of people died on the *Loch Ard*. Maybe all their ghosts got together to take the peacock back. Or superheroes? Thor could have smashed the case easy, and the Flash could have taken the peacock away so fast, no one could have seen him."

"This is stupid," I say, drifting back to the idea that Annabel is insane. "None of those suggestions makes any sense."

"Exactly," Annabel says with a smile. "So what are we left with? Someone very human, who stole the peacock in a way we haven't yet been able to work out. The only way we're going to solve this is by thinking logically—the kind of thinking that produced Pi. Now, we can sit here feeling sorry for ourselves, or we can examine what we know."

Annabel is right. I *have* been feeling sorry for myself. "Okay," I say. "Let's look at it rationally. But can we do it somewhere that sells Coke and French fries?"

Annabel laughs and stands up. "I know just the place."

is warbling away in the background. I'm halfway through my second Coke—I don't think the first one even touched the sides of my throat on the way down—and chomping through a plate of the best fries I've ever eaten.

I doubt Annabel wants me to answer her question, so I dip another fry in ketchup and keep eating. Sure enough, she goes on. "The last time we know the peacock was there for sure was about a half hour before Penny heard the crash. That was before the electricians left."

"Could the electricians have taken it? They had a truck parked out front." I like to think I'm contributing.

"Good idea." Annabel writes, *Electricians?* in her notebook. "Trouble is, we have two problems. One, they didn't carry anything as big as the peacock out the front door, or Penny would have noticed. And two, they left before the case was smashed."

Annabel puts another two question marks beside *Electricians?* "After the electricians left, there was only Pete and Penny. Penny was at the front desk except for when she went to the washroom, but we don't know where Pete was. Could he have stolen it?"

"Not on his own," I say. "Where would he put it?"

"Besides, Pete wouldn't need to smash the case—he has a key." Annabel puts Pete's name in the book but follows it with a question mark.

"So someone else," I suggest.

Annabel writes, *Someone else.* "Okay. Someone else comes in and steals the peacock, someone who was tipped off that the power on the alarms would be out."

"Pete could have tipped off his dad."

Annabel rubs her chin thoughtfully. "That doesn't sound like Kelly. It's not the way he works. I'm not certain that he and Pete are smart enough to pull off something this complicated. And, don't forget, Kelly was at the wreck with us when the peacock was stolen."

"He could still be involved," I say weakly.

"I suppose so." Annabel puts *Kelly* beside *Someone else* and adds the inevitable question marks.

"We've got an awful lot of question marks," I point out.

"I know," Annabel says. She chews the end of her pencil. "I don't see how we get around Penny hearing the crash. Even with her going back to her desk first, there's not enough time for anyone to get the peacock out, into a vehicle and away. I don't see how the timing can possibly work."

"So we're heading back to impossible."

"No. We're missing something."

We sit in silence for a few minutes. Annabel doodles in her notebook, and I finish off my fries. Annabel is drawing keys and locks. Suddenly, she stops. "You saw the lock for the peacock's case lying on the floor?"

"Yeah," I say, wondering why this is important.

"It hadn't been forced?"

"Didn't look like it. But whoever stole the peacock didn't need to force the lock. They simply went through the case with a club of some sort."

"Exactly. So why was the lock open?"

"It fell apart when the case shattered?" I suggest.

Annabel shakes her head. "It was a high-tech lock. You'd need explosives to get it apart without a key."

Realization dawns on me slowly. "So the case was unlocked with a key."

Annabel nods. "And then someone smashed it to make us think that was how the peacock was stolen. That solves our time problem. The thieves had a full half hour after the electricians left to remove the peacock. The peacock was long gone when the case was smashed."

"By Pete? Then he ran out onto the deck so that Penny wouldn't find him beside the smashed case," I suggest.

"Maybe," Annabel says thoughtfully. "That would explain why Pete only came in when he heard Penny scream, not when the crash happened."

"So Pete's the thief?" I say.

Annabel's brow furrows as she concentrates. "But he couldn't have worked alone, and we still have no idea how the peacock was removed. It wasn't taken to the road, and it wasn't hidden in the village. It couldn't have been carried very far—someone would have noticed, and there wasn't a lot of time."

Again we lapse into silence. I'm trying to imagine what happened.

I do my best imagining out loud. "The electricians leave," I say. "Pete lets his accomplices in and opens the peacock case. At least two accomplices take the peacock out the back, so Penny doesn't see them. Pete comes back into the museum, smashes the case and then goes out onto the deck. He probably assumed that Penny wouldn't hear the crash."

"She wouldn't have heard it if she'd been at her desk instead of near the washroom," Annabel says. "He probably intended for more time to pass before the theft was discovered. But when he heard Penny's scream, he had to go back in."

"So Pete's involved." I keep thinking aloud. "An international dealer is paying Pete, and maybe Kelly, to steal the peacock for him." Then another problem surfaces. "But how could someone in New York or wherever know there was going to be a storm last night that knocked out the power?"

"He didn't," Annabel says excitedly, the words tumbling out of her. "The plan was to steal the peacock at night. That's why Pete was so keen to work the night shift. That way he could power down the alarm system and have plenty of time to remove the peacock. They were ready to go, but they got tired of waiting and saw the power cut as an opportunity." She calms down and frowns. "Of course, this is all speculation, and it doesn't answer all the questions."

"So what do we do?"

Annabel closes her eyes. She has the look of concentration she has when she's reciting Pi. "If we're right and the thieves were taking advantage of the storm, I doubt they were ready to ship the peacock out of Warrnambool. It's still here, but it'll be gone soon, probably tonight." She opens her eyes and stares at me. "Is there anything else we could have missed?"

It's my turn to close my eyes as I run back through the events, from arriving at the museum to searching the village. Nothing jumps out at me until I remember sitting on *Reggie*, watching Pete as he smoked his cigarette on the dock.

"That's it!" I shout, startling Annabel and the waitress. "When we were on *Reggie*, Pete was on the dock across from us."

"Ye-es," Annabel agrees warily.

"His legs were dangling off the end of the dock. When you showed me the village yesterday, there was a red rowboat there. Today it was gone. Has anybody moved it?"

"I don't think anyone was at the pond today except us." Annabel sounds interested.

"Does the pond still link to the sea?" I ask.

"No, but it's only a short distance to the beach."

"Short enough that someone could haul a rowboat over it?" I ask.

"That's how they did it." Annabel is standing now. The alarmed waitress is staring. "Pete unlocked the case. The two accomplices took the peacock through the village, put it in the rowboat and took it out to sea. Come on! We have to get back to the museum. It'll be dark in a couple of hours, and then it'll be too late."

I follow Annabel out, smiling apologetically at the waitress.

"These wouldn't be here if they had been made before the storm," Annabel says, gazing out to sea. "This *has* to be where they dragged the red rowboat, with the peacock in it. But where did they go from here?"

"Not far in a rowboat. Do you think there was a larger boat waiting for them?"

"I doubt it. All of the places along this coast where you can dock something big are a day's sail away, so the boat would have had to head out in the storm, and way before the theft. They'll probably use today to get here and arrange to pick up the peacock tonight."

"It's just a guess," I say, "but maybe we should go to the police anyway."

"Ideally, yes," Annabel agrees, "but the police won't act urgently on a guess, and if we're right, the peacock will be long gone by tomorrow morning. It'll be on the open ocean, on its way to a display case in some rich collector's basement. So we've got to work out where it's being kept."

"Kelly's place?" I suggest.

"I doubt it. Kelly and Pete live on the landward side of town. It would be too much of a risk to unload and transport it through town and then reverse the process tonight. Kelly has a reputation, so the police might even be watching him. It's got to be stored somewhere close to the beach."

"You know the town better than I do. Can you think of anywhere?"

"It's not going to be in Warrnambool itself," Annabel says, "and there's not much round about, but there's a lot of coast to check. If only we could narrow it down."

It isn't exactly a lightbulb going on above my head—more like an electrical connection sparking as my brain links a bunch of different facts. "Is there a place between where we first met and the Mahogany Ship?" I ask.

Annabel thinks for a minute. "There's an old shack in the dunes about halfway between, but no one lives there. Kids use it for partying on the weekends."

"Anything else?"

Annabel shakes her head.

"I think the peacock might be there," I say.

"Why?"

"Percy."

"Percy?"

"Percy's owner, actually." I'm speaking slowly, because my mind is putting things together as I talk. "He doesn't fit in. Expensive suit and city shoes are not what you normally wear on the beach."

"We get a lot of strange tourists here," Annabel says, but I can tell she's interested.

"Okay, but when we met him yesterday afternoon, he told Percy they were going home, and yet he headed away from town," I point out. "This morning, he and Percy were walking along that trail, which has got to be a good two to three miles. He must be staying somewhere in between where we met and the Mahogany Ship. And you say that abandoned shack is the only place there is."

"You think he was there waiting for the peacock?" asks Annabel.

"It's possible," I say. "Maybe he's a collector who's decided to cut out the middle man. He sails here in his yacht and sets things up with Pete and or Kelly. He wants to keep an eye on what's happening, so he stays in the shack. Things are delayed, and then the storm comes along. The perfect opportunity. He tells Pete to go ahead, calls his yacht and waits for tonight."

"That's quite the story." Annabel shakes her head. "But we have no evidence."

"True, but it does explain the impossible," I point out. "And it means we don't have to involve aliens or superheroes. All of our guesses so far have been right."

"As far as we can tell, they have," Annabel says. I'm about to argue more, but she continues, "If we're right about the peacock leaving town tonight, the only way it can be stopped is by blocking every road and blockading the coast. Even if that's possible, there's no way we could convince the police to do it. We might be wrong, but it's our best guess and maybe our only chance to save the peacock."

"It wouldn't hurt to cycle out to the shack and check," I suggest. "If nothing's going on, we can pat Percy and come home."

"Okay," Annabel says. "Let's go before it gets dark."

I follow her back up through the village to pick up our bikes. Something I haven't said that's sitting in the back of my mind is, what if something *is* going on? What are we getting into?

Chapter Eleven

The sun is sitting on the western horizon by the time we reach the shack. It's almost hidden among the dunes, so we drop our bikes by the path and start walking toward it. On the ride here, we decided that playing innocent and walking right in is the best approach. We change our minds as soon as we see the red rowboat from the village nestled in dunegrass in front of the shack. We lie down behind a dune and watch.

"It looks deserted," Annabel whispers after a few minutes.

"It does," I agree. The shack is in better shape than I imagined. It's small, but the kids who use it to party obviously like their comfort. The roof is patched, and there's heavy, clear plastic nailed over the glassless windows. It looks as if it would be dry inside, but it can't have been much fun in the storm. There's a stack of empty bottles and beer cans against the wall. "Should we take a look?"

"I think one of us should," Annabel says. "The other can stay hidden and keep watch."

"I'll go," I say, with more chivalry than I feel. "If it comes to running away, I'll be faster than you would with your injured leg."

"That's rational," Annabel acknowledges. "Be careful, see if the peacock's there and hurry."

"Okay. And you phone for help if anything goes wrong," I add.

"There's no service out here," Annabel says matter-of-factly.

"Then cycle to where there is service and call." This idea seems worse and worse by the minute, but I'm committed now.

I climb over the dune, crouched low, and head for the shack, wishing I wasn't so rational. I peer through a side window, but it's hard to make out anything more than vague shapes through the grubby plastic. Nothing inside is moving. Hugging the rough wall, I creep around to the front of the shack.

The door opens easily, and I leave it open to let in as much light as possible. I'd expected dirt and spider webs, but the room is remarkably clean. Against one wall is a cot, a sleeping bag and pillow neatly laid out on top of it. In the middle of the room, there are a couple of chairs and a small table with an oil lamp and a briefcase sitting on it. The only other piece of furniture is a tattered green couch, and there's something on it— something about a meter and a half long, covered by a blanket.

I want to turn and run, but I have to be sure. I cross the room, kneel down and pull back the blanket. The head of the peacock looks up at me, its colors brilliant even in the dim light. That's when Percy barrels into me, knocking me over and licking my face. A voice from the doorway says, "At least one of us is pleased to see you."

I look up to see Percy's master smiling at me. In his left hand he's holding a small black pistol. The pistol is not pointed at me, but that doesn't make me feel much better. "Are you going to shoot me?" I ask.

"Shoot you? Heavens no. That would be uncouth. This"—he waves the pistol in the air—"is merely a precaution. I don't like to see doors open when I know I closed them." The man puts the pistol in his pocket. "I may tie you up until my business here is finished, but a resourceful boy such as you won't need more than a few hours to free himself. Where's your red-headed friend, by the way?"

"She's back in town," I say as calmly as I can manage. "We had an accident at the Mahogany Ship this morning, and she injured her leg." I hope that Annabel has seen the man arrive and is now getting help somehow.

"It looked like a dangerous place to me," the man says pleasantly. "I prefer to do my collecting in a civilized manner."

I drag myself to my feet, pushing Percy away. The dog instantly loses interest in me and rushes out the door.

If I can keep the man talking, perhaps I can edge toward him until I'm close enough to knock him down and run away. He doesn't look fit or strong. "You're one of those rich, crooked collectors," I say, taking a step forward.

The man smiles. "Rich, yes, but I don't like to think of myself as crooked. I have money—why not spend it on beautiful things?"

"Because you take beautiful things and hide them away where no one can see them and where experts can't study them."

The man laughs. "You're very young. You think that the alternative to my hoarding is a perfect museum where everything's displayed and available for an archaeologist to study whenever he or she wishes. It doesn't work that way.

Museums show only a fraction of what they have. The rest rots in back rooms because there is no funding to look after things. At least my collection is preserved."

I steal another step forward. "You're just a thief like any other." I expect the man to get angry, but he just smiles calmly.

"Oh, I don't know about that," he says. "I managed to save some very nice pieces in Baghdad before a mob rampaged through the National Museum and helped themselves to whatever took their fancy. Who knows what would have happened if I hadn't saved what I did?"

I'm close enough now. One quick leap and I'll be on him. I hear Percy bark somewhere outside. I'm steeling myself to jump when the man winks at me as if he can read my mind. I hesitate, and he turns and addresses someone behind him. "It's in here. Let's get it out to the boat."

The man steps outside, and two strangers duck through the door. Neither looks like someone I'd want to mess with. The shack seems suddenly crowded, and I back against the far wall. The men ignore me, pick up the peacock and leave.

I hear their voices outside. "The rollers are pretty bad."

"The Zodiac should handle them, but we don't want to overload her. Take the peacock out to the yacht and then come back. I've still got a couple of things to tidy up here."

"Right you are," one of the men replies. Percy barks again, and the same man says, "Can you keep that dog under control?"

There's silence for a moment, and then I hear, "Percy! Percy, come here!"

More silence, and then the man in the suit reappears in the doorway. "All's going well so far," he says cheerily.

"Sounds like Percy's not doing what he's told."

The man shrugs. "He's an enthusiastic puppy. Doesn't know the world yet. Much like yourself. Now, if you'd be so kind as to take a seat on the couch, I'd like to practice my knot tying."

I sit down, and the man moves over to the briefcase. He never takes his eyes off me as he bends to remove a coil of nylon cord from it. "I'll try not to cut off the blood flow, but I must tie you securely, and I'd like to do it before the light fades." The man moves toward me, twisting the cord between his pudgy fingers and smiling.

Chapter Twelve

Just as the man gets to point halfway between me and the door, we hear a soft voice outside. "3.141592653589793..."

"What?" The man steps back, eyes moving between me and the door. He looks momentarily confused. "Who's counting? Is that your lunatic girlfriend?" He smiles. "I hope I have enough rope."

He moves toward the door. A handful of sand flies at him, catching him full in the face. The man curses and stumbles back a step, raising his hands to his eyes. I lunge at him. We crash into the doorframe. My injured hand is caught underneath us, and I cry out in agony. Then Annabel is through the doorway, hauling the man's jacket over his head. The pistol flies out of his pocket and clatters against the wall.

Annabel stops. "I didn't know he had a gun."

"It's okay," I say. "It was in his pocket."

"That's all right then," Annabel says, kicking the man's legs so that he falls to the floor. He's shouting something through his jacket, but I can't make out what it is.

"You'll have to tie him up," I say, waving my bandaged hand, which has dark patches of new blood on it.

Together we manage to get the man's arms behind him. I sit on his shoulders while Annabel expertly ties his wrists together, runs the cord down and ties equally elaborate knots around his ankles. She fastens the end of the cord around the door handle. "He's not going anywhere," she says proudly as the man struggles to roll onto his side. She picks up his gun and examines it with interest.

"Well," the man says. "You've done a good job with the knots. I guess I'm going to find out if my high-priced lawyers are worth it."

"Nothing seems to bother this guy," I comment.

"You don't need to worry when you have more money than some European countries," Annabel says.

"Did you get service on your cell phone?" I ask.

"Yeah, just up the path. Only one bar, but I texted Bill."

"Texted?"

"I didn't want to risk losing service in the middle of a call. Besides, I don't have much battery left. Don't worry—Bill and I text all the time. He'll get it."

"I hope so. It's going to be a long night if he doesn't."

Percy's excited barking on the beach reminds us of the other two men. "How long will it take them to get out to the yacht and back?" I ask.

"Quite awhile. I saw the yacht's lights from the dune. It's a long way out. Let's go and see how they're doing."

I glance down at the tied man. He seems remarkably calm.

"He's not going anywhere," Annabel says.

The scene we see from the top of the dune could be something from a comedy sketch, and we'd laugh if the *Loch Ard* peacock weren't at risk. The two men are struggling to launch their Zodiac in the surf. Their task is made almost impossible by Percy, who is leaping around them, thinking it's all a wonderful game.

The men are cursing and waving wildly, which only excites Percy more. After one particularly wild swing, one of the men falls on the edge of the Zodiac just as a wave breaks. The Zodiac tips, and the bundle rolls out into the surf.

"The peacock!" Annabel shouts. We rush down the beach as fast as our injuries permit. I reach the peacock first. I grab one end of the bundle and hold on.

By this time the men have righted the Zodiac, and Percy is standing in the surf, trying to decide whether to continue his old game or come and see what I'm doing.

"Drop that and back away," one of the men shouts as they advance on me.

I'm about to obey when three shots ring out, almost deafening me. I spin around and see Annabel. In the last glimmer of twilight, she looks like some mythological goddess. Waves crash around her feet, her hair flies wildly, and her is arm raised to the heavens. She fires another shot into the sky.

The men hesitate for a moment, then turn and pile into the Zodiac. We watch as they force the boat through the surf and head out to sea.

"I've always wanted to do that," Annabel says.

"Okay, Annie Oakley," I say. "But now do you want to help me get the peacock out of the surf?"

Together we drag the treasure up above the tide line and then flop down on the sand. Annabel leans against me, and I wrap my arm around her shoulder. I'm soaked, hurting and still trying to wrap my head around everything that's happened in the last two days, but I'm happy.

"Do you think it's okay?" Annabel asks.

"I think so. It's wrapped in a heavy blanket, and it's survived worse."

"I suppose. Now Bill can advertise it as the museum piece that's survived two shipwrecks."

"What made you recite Pi outside the shack?" I ask.

"I needed to get him to turn around but not be on his guard, so I could throw the sand in his eyes. I find that reciting Pi tends to confuse people."

"No kidding," I say with a laugh.

We look up as the sound of a helicopter rises above the crash of the surf. Its powerful light is sweeping the beach.

"I guess Bill got your text," I say.

"Told you he would," Annabel says and then leans over and kisses me.

Chapter Thirteen

"I don't think I'll be able to adjust to life in Adelaide without these fries," I say. We are sitting in the diner in Warrnambool—my new favorite place in my new favorite town.

"I'll mail you some every week," Annabel says.

"Thanks," I say, with as much sarcasm in my voice as I can muster. It's been four days since the peacock theft, and Annabel and I have barely been out of each other's company for more than a few hours in all that time. Our injuries are healing. Annabel can almost walk without a limp, and although it'll be awhile before my fingernail grows back, both my finger and the cut on my palm are much better. "I'll miss you," I blurt out.

"And I'll miss you." Annabel reaches over and squeezes my good hand. "But I've been working on Bill to take me with him next time he goes on a trip to Adelaide, and he says there's always a job for you at the museum in the school holidays."

"Not the night shift."

"No." Annabel laughs.

"Do you think all the fancy lawyers will get the millionaire collector off the hook?" I ask.

"Billionaire, more like," Annabel says. "Bill says the police told him the man's name is Humphrey Battleford. Apparently, he comes from an old English family that can trace its ancestry, and money, back to Henry the Eighth. Battleford owns estates outside London, a mansion in California and houses all over the world, even one in Vancouver. Every room of every house is filled with valuable art. He travels the world buying antiques."

"And stealing them," I add.

"The police suspect so, but Battleford's clever. He never does the dirty work himself, and, as he said, he can afford the best lawyers. So, yeah, he'll walk free."

Battleford had been arrested at the shack the night we found him, but he got out on bail the next day. There was very little hard evidence against him. His yacht was in international waters, so they couldn't arrest the two guys who tried to take the peacock.

Battleford was keeping silent while his lawyers claimed that he was simply caught in the middle when persons unknown decided to use the shack he was in to store the stolen goods. He even had all the correct paperwork for his pistol. "Money seems to have its advantages," I remark.

"Indeed," Annabel agrees. "Bill also told me this morning that Battleford is offering to make a substantial donation to the museum if the charges go away. It might be best. It would mean Bill could afford to keep the security firm on."

"That would be good," I say. "Strangely, it's Pete I feel most sorry for. Kelly seems to be free and clear."

"I think he is. And Pete will be okay too. One of Battleford's lawyers is advising him. He's claiming to have lost the key and gone out the back when the electricians went."

"That's nonsense. It doesn't fit with what we know."

"Yes, but without hard evidence, it's not worth the effort of bringing serious charges against him. He'll likely be charged with negligence and get probation. After all, he's a minor player in the whole thing."

"True. So the world goes on as before."

"No, it doesn't." We look up to see Rose MacAuley striding through the diner toward us. She's a small, energetic woman with a mop of gray hair that never seems to be under control. "I thought I'd find you here," she says, sitting down in our booth. "I wanted to tell you something as soon as I could."

"What?" we both ask.

"The pot you found," Rose says. "I haven't finished working on it yet, but I have found something." She opens a huge purse, rummages for a moment and then brings out a small Ziploc bag, which she hands to us.

Annabel and I put our heads close together and peer at it. There's a coin in the bag, about the size of a quarter, but brown. It's badly corroded, and there's a hole in the center.

"Do you know what it is?" Rose asks enthusiastically.

"A coin?" I suggest.

"Exactly," Rose enthuses. "To be precise, a Chinese coin."

"So the pot was dropped by a Chinese laborer," Annabel says. "At least we'll get something to add to our exhibit."

"I think you'll have a whole new exhibit."

"What do you mean, Rose?"

"I mean," Rose says with a grin, "that when you examine the coin under a lens, you see writing. Chinese writing that places the coin in the Ming

117

Dynasty—specifically, the reign of the Xuande Emperor."

Rose looks at us triumphantly. We stare back blankly.

"The Xuande Emperor," Rose repeats to no greater effect. "I don't know what they teach you kids in school today," she says, shaking her head sadly. "The Xuande Emperor of the Ming Dynasty ruled China between 1426 and 1435. He sent Admiral Zheng He and his treasure fleet out on their final voyage."

Rose sits back and folds her arms. It takes a moment for what she has said to register. Then it hits us both like a ton of bricks. The Mahogany Ship is older than even the conspiracy theorists thought. The Chinese got to Australia almost two hundred years before the Dutchman Janszoon and more than three hundred years before Captain Cook.

"This'll change everything," Annabel says.

"Not everything," Rose says, "but a lot. I don't think there will be much difficulty getting funding to excavate the Mahogany Ship now. But I have to get back to the lab. The more coins I can clean up, the more persuasive the argument will be." She takes the Ziploc bag and stands. "This is such an exciting time to be an archaeologist."

"Wow," is all I can think to say.

"So, I guess our school holidays will be spent digging in the sand," Annabel says.

"I don't think anyone will be able to stop us." We laugh. Coming to Australia and Warrnambool were the best decisions my dad ever made.

Author's Note

There is considerable evidence that an unidentified shipwreck is buried in the sand dunes somewhere along the beach from Warrnambool. Theories as to its identity range from its being one of Zheng He's treasure ships to a lost Portuguese caravel to simply a lost fishing boat. Until a storm uncovers it, we'll never know.

The *Princess Sophia* disaster actually happened, as did the wreck of the *Loch Ard*. It is possible to climb down and visit the cave where Tom and Eva sheltered and drank brandy. Miraculously, the porcelain peacock did survive the wreck and does now sit in pride of place in the Flagstaff Hill Maritime Museum. However, it is probably much harder to steal than I suggest. I am also certain that the staff of the museum are much more professional and scrupulous than the fictional characters I placed there, and I apologize to them for not making them so. In the interest of the story, I have also taken liberties with the layout of the museum and placed the pond at the foot of the heritage village much closer to the water.

Other than that, the background is fairly close to reality, and I recommend a visit to the Shipwreck Coast and Warrnambool to anyone in the area.

John Wilson is the author of numerous novels for young people, all of them with historical themes. He lives in Lantzville, British Columbia.

orca *currents*

For more information on all the books
in the Orca Currents series, please visit
www.orcabook.com